@BucciCoin

Limited edition of 100.

Trickhouse Press
Dundee
June 2023

@Streetsweeper77

replying to @BucciCoin

This post has been removed
for breach of our Terms of Service

I think I'm ready for the man playing the chicken.

Do you really think you have behaved in a way deserving
of the man playing the chicken?

INTELLECTUAL PROPERTY CEASE AND DESIST

From

Alan M. Dershowitz
acting on behalf of my client
Dr. Thomas M. Tayler

Date: 22/01/2022

Re: Unauthorized Disclosure of Intellectual Property

Dear Madame/Sir Michael Josiah Sutton

We have reason to believe that you are in direct violation of revealing information that is deemed intellectual property of Dr. Thomas M. Taylor and Associates

The infringing actions include the following:

Use of language associated with $Buccicoin, $🍑 ,
$🍑🥴.

<u>IT IS REQUIRED THAT YOU CEASE AND DESIST THE FOLLOWING</u>:

All language and terminology associated with $Buccicoin.
Including the word Bucci and all associated representations of $Buccicoin.

If you fail to comply with the aforementioned demand(s) within 0.2 days we will have no choice but to pursue all legal causes of action, including but not limited to, the filing of a lawsuit to protect our interests. We remind you that this letter serves as a pre-suit notice for a lawsuit against you and failing to correct will likely make you liable for any damages the court determines we have suffered as a result of your infringement(s) including any reasonable attorneys' fees.

Sincerely,

@Complicatedangel

replying to @BucciCoin

I usually don't agree with stuff like this
but you talk a lot of sense but usually I
don't agree with stuff like this

How would you like to turn 1 BucciCoin into 10! BucciCoin?! Try our new Profit Accumulator with BucciCoin NOW! $*Bucci Coin*™ *is a registered trademark of Michael Josiah Sutton. Any attempts to reteritorialise $Buccicoin*™ *will be met with immediate civil action.*

I WILL KILL YOU FUCKER

BucciCoin exists to exist, like the locomotive.
Civilisation, ancient Egypt, the Roman empire.
Google it, hunter-gatherer 😌 BucciCoin exists!
Here are some images. This could be any city.
A city of BucciCoin, buildings moving smoothly
like the stage design on Catchphrase. This is
BucciCoin. It exists. Nothing you can do about it.

@6obelisk6

replying to @BucciCoin

I get you a razor you can do the job yourself

Remember a big thing used to be 'hot cheerleaders but scary and goth'.
Where did they go?

BucciCoin exists to STOP them targeting you
through your home appliances so you are NOT
lying in bed taunted by the chorus of Rob Zombie -
Dragula. You don't even know the words,
it's just noises. Boow dada da dam do booow
dada da da di booow dada da di da DRAG
YOU LUHH. They will tell you, 'Just go with it,
it could be your new thing, you could be
"the Dragula guy", we're willing to support you
through this difficult transition'. Don't listen
to them. Buy BucciCoin now, and sleep like a baby.

@DisgustedVoter44

replying to @BucciCoin

Yesterday I saw a beetle mating with a beer bottle
and I have to say I found it quite provoking.
I have been in a state of arousal ever since
but as soon as I saw your utter disregard for the
Rules-Based International Order
I shriveled up like a petal in the sun.
What even is 'splooshing'?
You should be ASHAMED of yourself.

@7875758493090

replying to @DisgustedVoter44

message me

You're saying I've had this microwave
psychological mind control targeting for decades
and it can all be cleared up with one tiny pill???
Grown used to it tbh. I fe3l I would actually miss
that that constant excruciating tone in my ear.
Keep your pills and your Havana Syndrome
Vaccine™ away from me. I'm happy as, Larry.

They're up to something.
None of this is real.

@NauticalNed

replying to @BucciCoin

WHAT IS THIS??? DON'T YOU KNOW
THEYRE STOCKPILING PORK
WEVE GOT TO THAT POINT BUT
YOURE GOING ON ABOUT THIS?
WHATS THE POINT OF THIS?
WHILE NEWS ARE ALL LIKE
(HAS) HE PLAYED A BLINDER
WITH THESE PROPOSALS AFTER
(WHAT SOME WOULD CALL)
A BARNSTORMING SPEECH(?)
SECOND TO NONE CRYPTOPARTIAL
REPORTING BEAUTIFUL TO WATCH
BUT THIS JUST HAS NOTHING
TO DO WITH IT DOES IT???

Do you feel like 20222 has already been longer than 2022?
How many hours has it been since 2009? give or take
a few for 'maintenance'? BucciCoin gives you access
to the ledger. You can pinpoint the exact moment you peaked.
Buy BucciCoin now. You know a chicken is born
with all the eggs it will ever lay inside of it. There's no proof
this isn't true of humans. Are you vegan? Do you want to see
an NFT of a man playing a chicken? It's an NFT!

Is this what our lives look like
when we finally escape the west?

@snugly_bubbles

replying to @BucciCoin

take my tie and tie it round your throat the fuckin
take you gokarting know what I mean and
fucking ram you off the track but if i werent in work
right now god knows but one days burden
is enough for one day mate

@Marco491

replying to @snuggly_bubbles

Quite right too

Bucci coin is just doing that meme now.

I am going to create
an environment that is so toxic,

This one.

😲

It's dark I know. But you can change everything if you invest in BucciCoin. What is BucciCoin? BucciCoin is a decentralised digital currency created in January 2022. It follows ideas set out in a white paper by Draxton Baylor. The identity of the person or persons who created the coin is unknown (for now). BucciCoin offers the promise of lower transaction fees than traditional online payment mechanisms. Unlike government-issued currencies, it is operated by a decentralised authority. BucciCoin is a popular token for customers of sex workers, fans of the band TOOL, online private sports betters, and people who purchase large quantities of silica traditionally used for cosmetic surgeries such as 'butt lifts' or 'butt cheek implants'. BucciCoin is known as a type of cryptocurrency because it uses cryptography to keep it secure. There are no physical BucciCoins, only balances kept on a public ledger which everyone has transparent* access to (although each record is encrypted). All BucciCoin transactions are verified by a massive amount of computing power via a process known as 'splooshing'. BucciCoin is not issued or backed by any banks or governments (yet!). BucciCoin is commonly abbreviated to $🍑 when traded or $🍑😝 on popular social media websites. Invest in BucciCoin TODAY! 1 $🍑 = £37, 895.54p. This is a once in a lifetime opportunity to get in on the ground floor of THE FUTURE.

NERRRRRRD!

@arrogantmrjesus

replying to @BucciCoin

stab stab stab
stab stab
stab stab stab stab stab stab stab
stab
stab stab stab stab not stab human
nature stab stab
conspire stab
population
stab stab stab stab stab stab stab
stab stab stab nagging stab
stab stab and stabstab stab stab
I got stab it I want stab it got stab stab
stab stab stab stab
stab stab stab stab
stab not stab stab
stab stabstab stab
human stab
stab remember stab stab
stab when we used to stab stab
stab stab stab stab
stab stab stab stab stab
natural thing stab is stab
not stab and stab in fact stab
quite stabstab stab
stab stab stab stab
stab stab stab stab stab stabs stab
conspire as stab in stab
breathe stab stab stab stab
together stab stab television stab
when the industry does a stab
we stab stab
stab stab stab stabs stab
stab stabs stab stab stab stab
stab stab stabs stab a review stab
a review of a stab
very good stab with stab a stab
conspire as in stab together stab the stab
psst stab in a stab stab stab
yes stab when you stab it yes stab

BucciCoin is a British institution.

But who is the most British person?

Flick through all the names in your head and you will see the person who sits directly in the middle of Britishness and what it is to be British is Danny Mills.

Yes, this is the only sensible answer.

I have ehad enough of this CUNT!

@NooneInparticular

replying to @BucciCoin

On the other hand, if you shaved them
and stuck googly eyes over their skin
they would probably seem a lot less alien.
I cultivated a large aspidistra once,
I tickled it and talked with it frequently,
and within a very short period of time
I came to know it as a friend. Perhaps
if we took a similar tact with these 'coins'
perhaps we might not be in this mess
in the first place. Just my opinion.

Do you remember when that cruel boy in school
hurt himself running directly into your shoulder
so he cried and shouted, Can't you just get out
of my way? This seemed to ignite a deep hatred
for you which was later evidenced when the pretty
girl with glasses stole his diary and read you
several entries specifically about how he definitely
hates you. He is probably going to murder you
one day. And remember when you were shielding
the ball on the playground and he shouted,
Obstruction! Obstruction! and gave himself
a freekick? That boy is investing in BucciCoin
right now. You want him to get in on the ground
floor of THE FUTURE ahead of you? No.
Invest in BucciCoin now while prices are LOW.
Bucci coin is the official cryptocurrency of
Shrewsbury Town FC. Come on the Shrews!

I feel like this picture really defines a lot of what my life is all about.

@rainwateronice

replying to @BucciCoin

and did you see that video of them
bringing down that massive
lamppost outside BucciCoin HQ wow
one of those whish I was there
moments fucking amazing

2023 is here. To EVERYONE, including all haters and losers, HAPPY NEW YEAR. Work hard, be smart, and always remember, WINNING TAKES CARE OF EVEYTHING! Put on Louis Prima – Buona Sera and dance! 20223 is the year of BucciCoin. 20 years ago today Triple H came back from his quad injury dressed in one of the most iconic outfits of all time: denim vest over leather jacket, bootcut jeans. I know this was a very formative experience for you. BucciCoin believes in you. BucciCoin believes you could pull off that look. All you have to do is believe in BucciCoin too! Now, dance to Louis Prima and do Sambuca shots out of your own belly button. Shine! Do NOT let life pass you by! Buy low, sell high. . . Time to play the game [*feverish laughter*]

happy new year brother x love u 4ever x

I made this especially for you. It's an NFT.

StephenPierce421

replying to @Complicatedangel

Yes, I have your diary.
I also have your ticket
for Tchaikovsky piano concerto no.1
next Thursday. I told you about it
ages ago. I've spent the last two months
getting the appropriate qualifications
so please don't let me down.

News just in: BucciCoin is now the official partner of Alpha Con 2023 where every variety of facial hair is represented, the fuzzy mask, the 1980s NASCAR driver goatee. Come and see 'Jimmy Rex', 'Nick Santonastasso', star attraction 'The Bull', and many more Alphas at Alpha Con 2023, LIVE from the Grand America Hotel. Be GREAT OR BE NOTHING. Be sure to purchase all your supplementary books and courses with BucciCoin (discounts available). Take your business to the next level at Alpha Con 2023:

March 18-19, 555 Main St, Salt Lake City, UT 84111 NOW! 🍑 😝

And MORE! You can now use BucciCoin as your token of choice in @NFTrackRacing, now available in beta. You can race against Big Muncher, Uncle Nasty, and other NFT horses from the Bucci Stable. Tournaments, jockeys, NFT horse breeding, performance boosting and more to come! Grab your NFT horse and let's race! @NFTrackRacing user @inthesadle1 rightly states: 'People don't like change, but if you don't change you get left behind and miss oportuntities like this to make life more comfortable in th future'. Obliterate the past, use BucciCoin with @NFTrackRacing today!

@SilkyLittleBumHair

replying to @BucciCoin

Dear sir/madame/etc.

Firstly, let me commend you
on your semantic shift in the sixth sentence
of your polemic. This had the rare effect
of taking me by surprise. The emotional
response you elicited was far beyond
that of your average rhetorical shock,
and the propulsion created towards
the barnstorming climax of your post
provided a much-needed lubricant
for the meat of your argument.
Your research appears to be thorough
but on the off chance there is a gap
in your knowledge I would like to direct you
towards the work of J. Simons Frith
whose hypothesis on the psychogeneses
of the 'chicken coop killers' may be of some use
to your continued explorations into cryptocurrency.
The work in question appears in 64:3 of The Whippet
I wish you all the success in the world.
Have a nice weekend.

Yours sincerely,

SilkyLittleBumHair

There is no god but God.

Due to recent reports linking BucciCoin with certain 'QAnon' conspiracy theorists, $Buccicoin™ (🍑) would like to make the following statement:

BucciCoin is not nor has ever been associated with 'interdimensional slugism' and has no public opinion on 'the Kennedys' or 'JFK Jr'. BucciCoin has no reason to believe that the amplification of narratives surrounding JFK Jr signals 'junk conspiracy implanted by the CIA'. All roads do not 'lead back to JFK'. The CIA are not 'eternally obfuscating' around this issue. BucciCoin denounces all sceptical thinking surrounding official narratives. BucciCoin (and affiliates) does not believe that the QAnon 'JFK Jr narrative' is the perfect way to malign any conspiratorial theories surrounding the 'assassination of JFK' by linking the 'JFK conspiracy' to the 'ultimate weirdos' of political culture. The fact that 'QAnon' is an incredibly easy group to infiltrate has no bearing on the matter. There is no evidence to suggest that the CIA can 'octopus-style' simultaneously provoke internet-based undercultures while still having a firm grasp on mainstream media. This is not 'terrifying'. Nor does BucciCoin have any public opinion on recent 'UFO (UAP) ops'. There is no evidence to suggest that 'painting noted CIA disinformation officers (who are still working for the government) as truth-seekers and planting UFO threat narratives on the front pages of popular newspapers' indicates any malicious intent. It cannot 'only get worse', and they have not 'brainwashed 90% of researchers'. All roads do not lead back to JFK. BucciCoin has no public opinion on whether 'Garrison landed on the US Aerospace industry as his key culprit'. BucciCoin (and affiliates) does not suspect the two are 'heavily linked'. BucciCoin is a decentralized digital currency with no political agenda. Become a member of the BucciCoin family now.

Thank you.

@poorprinceharry
replying to @BucciCoin

Hit them in the pockets

It is so peaceful here I love it. Peace and love. ✌️🌟❤️🎶🍒🌈🥦☮️

There are currently three 'woman breastfeeds cat on airplane' stories in the 'media'. Is this a real thing? How long has this been going on for? Does this confirm the existence of witches? How has this taken so long to come out?

You know the rule, if it fits under the seat in front of you, you can breastfeed it.

This needs serious investigation.

@Inanidealworld

replying to @BucciCoin

The next initiation is vital. No need to repent.
I find this equal parts disturbing and invigorating.
I feel it gets to the core of the GREAT CHAMGE
that is coming (any day now). Dogs will turn to wolves,
men will tremble as the merciless net swipes down
from the clouds. But I did find this quite disgusting I
suggest you moderate your language in future.
Though there is little future left. The collector
of purulence is weaving his fabric as we speak!
I turned the page and saw the words 'The Cat'
and through the windows closed I heard the wild
feline screeching. How many more signs do we need?

Now. . . BucciCoin [. . .] commemorative BucciCoin coins, to be precise
[. . .] five thousand BucciCoin, nine thousand BucciCoin, thirty thousand,
it all added up to just over eighty-four thousand (84,230) BucciCoin.

That BucciCoin is a significant amount of BucciCoin.

Every time I ring it goes to voicemail [. . .]
. . . minting costs. . . charges from the issuing authority
all they wanted was to sell you some more [. . .]
approximately five thousand BucciCoin p/h.

Get Paul on the line. Paul, the crypto-numismatist.
[. . .] the customer may still incur a loss
despite favourable price movement [. . .] sorry mate,
you keep breaking up there a bit. . .

Three-dimensional digital image correlation to quantify deformation and crack-opening displacement in ductile aluminum under mixed-mode I/III loading

Michael A Sutton

'Michael "Arsehole" Sutton'

@CaptinTincap

replying to @Streetsweeper77

wellho wdyouli keitifsomeo necom esinure
bathroo manble wtheholepla ce uplike
itwasfuck inworoldw ar3 theres2of
themanyway soit snotlikenoonsg onnamiss
thethingwhateve ritwasyouknow

[10:11]

Is it Taylor or Tayler? Tallyho?

[10:13]

Tallywacker. I mean, Tayler.

[10:22]

Wait what do you need
my name for?
Has this entire
conversation been a data
collection exercise?
Are you going to disappear
now and I have to pay
thirty thousand BucciCoin
to see my name in some
MIT social science
directory? If this has
anything to do with
transcendental meditation
I take back the name
I gave you
and urge you to
consider whether you
want to be a part of this.

[10:30]

Dear Mr. Talcumpowder,
your information has
been recorded and your
suitability for transcendence
will be analysed in due
course. Thank you for your
participation in this process.

What is BucciCoin?

@NauticalNed

replying to @BucciCoin

This comment has been removed
for breach of our Terms of Service

But we're not abandoning our roots. See the roofs?

Remember when Everton Brow was entirely Georgian Houses?
Unfortunately the government had to knock them all down
because communism was taking root. Not to worry, BucciCoin
is offering a special series of NFTs! for the people of Liverpool,
you can OWN your very OWN pre-demolition Georgian house,
numbers 1-862. People of Liverpool OWN your OWN
little piece of the forgotten past with BucciCoin NOW!

@HaIrYsMoKeR

replying to @BucciCoin

No mention of agrifoods?

The number of times I've been knocked over by one of those 'electronic cars'. Silent killers. That Musque fella is gonna have a lot to answer for in the next few years. Mark my words. But seriously get in touch with him. We could really do with a Musque pumpanddump?

Google

Trending searches

- putin russia ukraine
- jurassic world dominion official trailer
- samsung galaxy s22 ultra
- lassa fever virus
- national lottery lotto results
- kurt zouma cat west ham
- adidas sports bras bare breasts

Demented Nation.

Where is BucciCoint?!

ObviouslyAnonymous999

replying to @BucciCoin

GROWING UP AT THE SIDE OF
CHAIRMAN MAO THE RED SUN
RISES FROM SHAO SHAN
I AM A SUNFLOWER UNDER THE
SHINING FIVE STAR FLAG LITTLE
RED GUARDS ATTEND A REPUDIATION
MEETING CRITISIZE LIN PIAO AND
DISCREDIT HIM COMPLETELY LITTLE
RED GUARDS GROW STRONGER
IN THE FIGHT GOOD NEWS HAIL
FROM EVERY CORNER FORWARD
ON THE MAY SEVENTH ROAD
ILL GO TO THE BORDER REGION
TOO WHEN I GROW UP

Yeah, as if I would see that then instantly search adidas sports bras bare breasts and scroll through the results int he toilets at BucciCoin HQ. Ha. What a bunch of freaks.

Why have women turned the back on the bra (2022)?

Why has the oldest pub in Britain (1,229 years old) recently closed?

MrCompromise

replying to @BucciCoin

blahblahblah well on it with seventeen of them
probably with it was nevergonna happen but
let's not speculate there'snothing to fear it's not
my job to come and tell you what to to do your
acting up stop bandying it about apparently it's
worth twelve billion so I'm not scared to say
these things who knows I know they've been
having preliminary discussions but I don't want
people getting a false sense of what's going on
on I have a responsibilityto tell you about things
like life expectancy going down you can't explain
it there's not a single explaination fkrnit try Ila's
you might this is not our country but can you
explain to those of us who haven't followed it
how mnahwy points I need to get we use it to
benefit us we're a nation 20 billion people this
is just temporary you gotno idea what you're
talking about your light bulbs broke pal better
go back to school put it back down my colleague
was right about you hahaha the whole point of it
and that's become associatedwith artificial rain
now so you can't get what you want 9 times out
of ten I honestly don't think olive thought this
one through better go back to the drawing board
a total nonsense it doesn't apply to nine people
out of 10 I don't like to usethis word and I try
not to but yeah that's what we're worried about
that is the huge debate going on is an image of
a fetus graphic does that count yeah it's the inside
of a woman but it's medical so seems hypocritical
I would listen to the proper professionals on this

Talking to normies for 30 minutes
A three hour conversation with $🍑coiners

BucciCoin exists.